BACK TO THE FUCHSIA

T. S. IDIOT

BACK TO THE FUCHSIA

T. S. IDIOT

palavro
PUBLISHING

Back to the Fuchsia
By Tom Stockley

Copyright © Tom Stockley

IBSN: 978-1-912092-26-0

First published in 2024
by Arkbound Foundation (Publishers)

No part of this publication may be reproduced, stored in a retrieval system, or transmitted, in any form or by any means without the prior permission of the publisher, nor be otherwise circulated in any form of binding or cover other than that in which it is published and without a similar condition being imposed on the subsequent purchaser.

Arkbound is a social enterprise that aims to promote social inclusion, community development and artistic talent. It sponsors publications by disadvantaged authors and covers issues that engage wider social concerns. Arkbound fully embraces sustainability and environmental protection. It endeavours to use material that is renewable, recyclable or sourced from sustainable forests.

Arkbound
Backfields House
Upper York Street
Bristol, BS1 8QJ

www.arkbound.com

For Sticky, Jules & Tom

— your weird, bright lights still sparkle.

INTRODUCTION   1

prologue
DOG POEM   3

12:00
FRAGMENTS OF A PINK PLASTIC PLATE   5
SADNESS IS A GIFT   7

13:00
NOTES ON A BROKEN SHOWER   8
EULOGY FOR A DEAD CAT   10

14:00
WALK OF SHAME AS A RELIGIOUS EXPERIENCE   12
PLASTIC BAG   14

15:00
YOU, A PUDDLE   15
JONI MITCHELL MOMENT   16

16:00

MINE / YOURS	17
MOUNTAIN ENERGY	19

17:00

ICARUS IN RIPPED JEANS	21
FRONTIERLAND	22

18:00

HOPSCOTCH TO NOWHERE	23
STRANGE POWERS	24

19:00

SELF-PORTRAIT AS A SEA PINK	26
OCEAN CITY (OUT GETTING RIBS)	28

20:00

MY LONELINESS IS KILLING ME	29
POEM	30

21:00

WET FAG, FUTILE GESTURES   31
DISCO BOYFRIEND   32

22:00

LAST TWINK ON EARTH   33
GODLESS PLACE   35

23:00

SAG HARBOR, LONG ISLAND   37
הָכָר (A BLESSING)   40

00:00

THERE WILL BE SORROW   41
A CENSORED SEXT   43

epilogue

BACK TO THE FUCHSIA   44

ACKNOWLEDGEMENTS   46

INTRODUCTION

People know me mostly for my loud, fast and (subjectively) funny punk poetry—but I wrote most of these poems when there was nothing to laugh about and everything was silent. Between 2019 and 2024, when the world fell apart, so did I.

These poems were the start of my attempt to cultivate resilience. To find tenderness in tragedy. To feel something, still. To look back on my life, knowing it hasn't been wasted, and to move forwards knowing that a future exists.

Back To The Fuchsia is a collection of everyday moments (in all their sadness and small joys) presented in a 12-hour window—modern myths unravelled and expressed through gut-feeling, ephemeral echoes from a life unfiltered and tenderly observed. These words came from my wanders through the council estates, cityscapes, and crumbling coastlines that I have called home.

These are my thoughts on the people and places that permeate our lives and the paths we take to find them— from dead cats and plastic bags to houseplants and corner shops; muddy reflections on class, queerness and community from someone who's doing their best.

Speak them aloud and let them linger.
I wrote them for you.

DOG POEM

you are
a benevolent shadow

you are endless devotion
and a wet smell

you are a breath of stale air,
shared with utter joy

you make mornings
great again

you make leaving
ache again

you are hope,
personified

to you it's always
dinner time

you would walk
in any weather

you make every
setback better

you are daylight
in a deluge

you are dog,
and i love you.

12:00
morning / mourning

FRAGMENTS OF A PINK PLASTIC PLATE

I woke up thinking of you, again,
an appendicitis pain
that sits between my ego
and the bag of all your things
left behind the bedroom door
in the hope that you'll come back.

The second thing I did today
was drop my favourite plate
(bamboo plastic, pale pink)
and watch it fall towards the floor
with terminal velocity and
become fragments at my feet,
serrated edges cutting the space
that used to hang between us.

You always knew what to do with our day
and now I make breakfast for one.

SADNESS IS A GIFT

I am remembering how to cry
for the first time in years.

Sitting here and sobbing,
sorrow seeping from my skin
like post-storm sea foam.

Houseplants are wilting, mourning as I am
—sadness is a gift.

13:00
everything in my house is dead

NOTES ON A BROKEN SHOWER

Patient: T.S.
Ward: Mason Unit (Section 136)
11.10.21

naked, I was met
with a lack of enthusiasm
as you faltered between dead cold and scalding
so I turned you off and on again
hours after attempting
to do the same for myself.

Steam rose from pale limbs,
proof of life (or something like it)
as I shared space with the run-off
from another person's sacred routine,
with scents of nights and days spent
in a wilderness of safety.

I prepare myself to manifest
a destiny of wet socks and panic,
take stock of soap-embalmed surroundings
as someone else's pubic hairs congregate in the drain,
a mecca for the strands they had to spare.

I leave with their likeness on my mind
and no one to drive me home.

EULOGY FOR A DEAD CAT

made from words on a packet of cat food that she'll never eat

You are food for cats since 1958.
You are everything we do,
you are a whole journey.
You are spirit and you are instinct,
you are feline.
You are a stage of life
and you are every change.
You are 12 x 100 grams
of devotion.
You are *the good stuff*.
You are strong defences
and a soft touch.
You are balanced mineral levels,
you are complete, and you are love.
You are no fillers,
you are no nasties.

You are tins, pouches, pots and treats.
You are an encore.

14:00
it's cold outside

WALK OF SHAME AS A RELIGIOUS EXPERIENCE

With chipped nails I stagger past
a two-headed man in a pin-striped suit
and hang over myself
under a hot pink sky

as seagulls defecate on statues,
polythene bags shelter in the shadows
like cattle that no longer produce milk,
emaciated and ready to be culled.

And as we book Airbnb rooms
in sick and dying cities,
we know that we are beautiful,
we know that we are doomed.

Olivia Newton John takes her last breath
at the exact moment I go into overdraft.

I am walking to therapy
and I do not know where to start.

PLASTIC BAG

after Katy Perry

An eco-friendly carricr bag
takes a week to break down
—I wish I could last that long
without decomposing
to pieces.

15:00
as the rain falters

YOU, A PUDDLE

You told me
that you were
                a puddle of
oil,
meaningless in your muddiness.

I told you that in every drop
                          of us
there's a prism of colours,
reflecting our true form.

JONI MITCHELL MOMENT

A swollen river
full circle
(life in no motion)

16:00
mines & mountains

MINE / YOURS

this used to be a mining town
where houses built like rotting teeth
were warmed by coal,
black gold from chiselled wounds
beneath laboured feet
on ancient lines.

men have died here
and I have tried too.

now the mines are flooded
with hot water from below
geothermal energy that
heats these homes once more.

it is possible to harness heat,
and find hope,
from your scars.

MOUNTAIN ENERGY

after Mark E. Smith
Benidorm, 2023

I lift rocks on Spanish mountains
while my mother brushes her teeth.

A father tells stories of football
over the menu of the day.

The last few snakes from the summer heat
crawl across discarded bathroom floors.

Ten televisions, scattered on a wasteland,
make transmissions of Earth not yet received.

The bones of a cat's foot
speak to me from the dust in which they rest.
Patriotism is the last refuge, they say

as you catch me, and we kiss
on the concrete of a half-built condo.

17:00
discomfort zones

ICARUS IN RIPPED JEANS

I haven't moved an inch in hours,
too afraid to disturb the bouquet
that I left on myself
when I thought that I'd stopped breathing.

Sat in a paint-smeared chair,
the astroturf beneath my feet
littered with pigeon shit and dog ends,
I feel gorgeous, briefly.

No one can kick me down further
than I have bought myself
but still I rise;
Icarus in ripped jeans.

FRONTIERLAND

The 4pm frontier is here again,
veneer of spit and sawdust-speckled
moments of a day that won't forgive.

Tasks completed, medicated,
body washed and dressed,
but still the horrors come for me;
relentless, awful shudders
in my stomach and my skull.

In the big Asda, I am nothing,
the limited potential of what I can be
glaring in the tiny screens
of the self-service checkout.

Why do I always
forget to bring a bag?

18:00
too late to apologise

HOPSCOTCH TO NOWHERE

I walk along cracked tarmac
towards being someone for myself
and anyone for you.

Under my feet,
a half-finished hopscotch grid,
childhood game reaching halfway
to a future that's no longer ours.

I've just eaten the worst sandwich of my life
and I miss you.

STRANGE POWERS

after Stephin Merritt

I've got strange powers,
tear ducts like Apple Sourz
viscous and cheap,
only served in moments of weakness.

The last time I cried was in a psychiatric ward
because I could hear nothing but myself
and before that, a birthday party,
Where I could only hear everyone else.

My tears are scratch card flakes
that land on pavement cracks

They are droplets that gather
in the styrofoam cups of AA meetings
They are old pound coins
left in dimly lit laundrettes

They are ketchup smears
and home-dyed hair

They are shopping lists in neon squares,
post-it notes to hold your love.

19:00
homesickness

SELF-PORTRAIT AS A SEA PINK

I grew up along this coastline,
a life behind the seaside scenes;
I did not share the sun-bleached memories
of those who come here just to leave.

Days did not play out in polaroids
or midsummer nightclub dreams;
this love was not part of their postcard,
printed pictures of what could have been.

And as the sea glass gives its glow
between cigarettes and bottle caps;
she stood between the wild tundra
of broken steps and boarded flats:

A Sea Pink, Armeria maritima,
still waiting for the waves
to tell her what it's worth.

OCEAN CITY (OUT GETTING RIBS)

after Basquiat

from misted plastic windows
comes the carcass of a fishing boat
lying in the salty flats—it welcomes me
and whispers nothing
and my concrete soul sighs sweetly
as it searches for itself
among the pleasant ruins
of the Ocean City's ribs.

20:00
pathetic fallacy

MY LONELINESS IS KILLING ME

after Britney Spears

my loneliness is killing me //
yet sometimes my friends come too
from sticky floors and plastic feelings //
fuchsia and afraid
our phones are silent,
out of sight //
Sambuca shots
and neon lights //
I still believe
that you'll be here //
hit me one more time.

POEM

A cheap moped falls in a car park
but no one's there to hear it,
so I don't know if it happened.

Later that night, I crouch,
gather shards of broken mirror
with gentle palms because I know
there's life in these reflections.

21:00
all of my tomorrows

WET FAG, FUTILE GESTURES

trying to roll a cigarette in the rain,
a vague attempt to fumigate
the anxieties I know too well
and get the upper hand
on the ones I haven't met yet.

lost bodies, latent love
and every paradise that we forgot,
every leaf that fell
from that neglected bonsai tree,
green tinged ghosts of a life half lived.

the taste of consequence in my mouth
is nothing new.

DISCO BOYFRIEND

o, disco boyfriend,
glitter clad and sweat drenched
you shimmer, cheap prosecco
tremors on the dancefloor
mirror-splintered luminescence
moonlit gay boy magic;
even the way you vomit
is tender and considered.

I would walk you home
in any weather.

22:00
late night stories

LAST TWINK ON EARTH

I am
the last twink on earth,
and I am tired.

I am
treading across broken glass on cathedral floors as
Furbies stare at me with lifeless eyes,
modern gargoyles with plastic teeth.

I am
wading through rivers of effluent,
greeting traffic cones and condom wrappers
as they float past towards better futures.
I am
crushing up my medication into lines and
breathing it into my nostrils, an acrid celebration.

I am
drinking poppers from the bottle
remembering all the nights I'll never taste
as the back of my throat burns sweetly.

I am
chewing on country and western vinyl records
salvaged from the burned out husk of a charity shop

I am
wandering, lonely as a chemtrail
as the post-apocalyptic air
soothes my skin.

GODLESS PLACE

Stumbling, wounded heron-like
along the banks of the canal
knowing I'm too drunk to dream
but not enough to bury my self-doubt.

I open Grindr, gaze into its chasm
of desire and damnation.
It is a godless place
for sacred opportunities.

He is 45, *discreet,*
and just around the corner
I know that hell is too, but I've already been there
so I send a message
—we both know what we want

Meet me in 15 minutes, I know a place.

Him in sports wear (no pants)
and me in rags of masculinity,
baseball cap and jeans.

Crisp leaves underfoot say more
than small talk ever could
as we slide our way into a hallowed purgatory,
to *that* clearing in the park.
We are sacred apparitions, in fear of being seen
but no hope of being found.

Our interaction is brief,
elastic snaps and mouthparts move
strangely formal *thanks* are made
and we part ways.

I feel tender with the weight of
wilted petals in dirty water
as I make my way back home.

23:00
naked, you saved me

SAG HARBOR, LONG ISLAND

after Ray Johnson

soles touch water,
waves lap at pale ankles
and I am

a happy meal
with its smile removed

salt water up to my waist,
thighs shake
and I am

a bruised sternum,
making a wish

leaning forward,
body buoyant
and I am

a boiled egg,
left unwanted in the saucepan

muscles arc,
tender is the flesh
and I am

a motorway,
made only of hard shoulders

soft hands propel me,
swimming out to sea
and I am

a Barbie girl
in an Oppenheimer world

lying backward,
held by the swell
and I am

free, here
I am

floating.

הָכָר (A BLESSING)

I have seen you spill your love on concrete,
sharp tongued and radiant.

I have heard your call,
a Camden queen on Cornish soil
and it has saved me.

I have seen the light of your being
when I have been in darkness.
I have known only your miracles.

Beloved between tides
and blooming, bastard skies,
our pale hands held close.

Beneath orange trees and echoes, always
your holiness I've known.

00:00
an end

THERE WILL BE SORROW

an ode to premiere stores

it's midnight on a thursday and
hot air scratches loud on tower blocks,
the sky's half-hearted revelry
that walks the line between
sorrow and small joys.

a weekly ritual takes me through the underpass
between the sofa and the corner shop,
the one that spills out onto the street
allowing the thirsty and committed
to nurse their late-night vices.

I pass empty cans and plastic packets
in the subway's luminescence,

cigarette gasps to a stub as I ascend the concrete steps
at the exact same moment as last week,
walking right through my own ghost.

I discard the blackened filter to its fate
among the other useless things,
enter the piss-yellow glow of the shop,
a temple of pleasure with no gods in sight
but me, the patron saint of tender feelings.

I crack the can before I'm home,
late to a party that never starts
— that the world would drown its sorrows
as quietly as I drink mine.

A CENSORED SEXT

          lying arms
push over,
holding your   pillow
         around me
your shoulders
         standing there,
inside.

Epilogue
(still awake)

BACK TO THE FUCHSIA

there will be a world
where people pray
in the wake of our pink dust
where we make lipstick traces
and dance like Ian Curtis
where we hold our own hands
and love like no one hurt us
we'll dig dirt beneath the fuchsia flowers
where somewhere else is always here
I promise you, queer darlings,
we will find our way back here.

ACKNOWLEDGEMENTS

Thank you to everyone who's mentored me, shared a stage with me, given me a chance, loved me and been loved by me, hurt me, held me, and hoped for better things with me.

Thank you to Arkbound, Literature Works, and The Literary Consultancy for believing in these words and their support throughout the creative process. Thank you to the editors at Renard Press who first published *you, a puddle* in their Kinship anthology (2023).

Thank you to Rosie Garland and Simon Barraclough for casting their expert eyes over these words and helping to make them their best.

Special thanks to my actual family, my poetry family (especially Bridget, Mal, Chris and Aish), Kez and Sylv, Cat, Aimée, Ruairí and Polly. Thank you for holding me when I couldn't hold myself.

Dedicated, most of all, to my nephew Fin, Peggy the dog, and every baby, lizard and bug I have ever known and loved. You're the reason(s) I'm still here.

ABOUT THE AUTHOR

Since 2013, Tom has been writing and performing across the UK, as well as working closely with community groups and young people. As a writer and artist they have produced work for BBC Arts, UNESCO and The Tate. In 2023 their short film Salt In The Wounds was shortlisted for the national Outspoken Prize for Poetry in Film and their short play All The Things I Said was shortlisted for the Pomegranate Theatre Prize. They have had work previously published in anthologies by Howling Press, Perennial Press, Renard Press and Ample Collective (among others).